T

D1716619

TREES

REDWOOD TREES

John F. Prevost
ABDO & Daughters

Published by Abdo & Daughters, 4940 Viking Drive, Suite 622, Edina, Minnesota 55435.

Printed in the United States.

Cover Photo credits: Peter Arnold, Inc.
Interior Photo credits: Peter Arnold, Inc.

Edited by Bob Italia

Library of Congress Cataloging-in-Publication Data

Prevost, John F.
    Redwood Trees / John F. Prevost.
      p. cm. -- (Trees)
    Includes index.
    Summary: Provides basic information about the redwood, including its structure, economic uses, and the pests and diseases that affect it.
      ISBN 1-56239-617-X
    1. Redwood--Juvenile literature. [1. Redwood.] I. Title. II. Series: Prevost, John F. Trees.
    QK494.5.T3P74 1996   96-6069
    585'.2--dc20   CIP
                                                                                AC

ABOUT THE AUTHOR
John Prevost is a marine biologist and diver who has been active in conservation and education issues for the past 18 years. Currently he is living inland and remains actively involved in freshwater and marine husbandry, conservation and education projects.

Contents

Redwood Trees and Family

Redwood trees are the tallest and largest living plants. Redwood tree **fossils** have been found worldwide. The tallest coast redwood was 372 feet (113 meters). Found in Humboldt Redwoods State Park, it fell in 1991.

Redwoods are named for the color of their beautiful wood. Younger trees are grown and cut for their **rot-resistant** timber.

Redwoods are **coniferous** trees. They are closely related to the **bald cypress**.

There are three types of redwood trees: the coast redwood, the sequoia (suh-KWOY-ah) redwood, and the dawn redwood. All are among the tallest trees in the world.

Redwoods get their name from their beautiful, red wood.

Roots, Soil, and Water

Redwood trees pull water from the ground with their roots. Water contains **minerals** and other **nutrients** which the tree uses for food. Without enough food, the tree will not grow or make seeds.

The roots also keep the tree from falling over. But the roots do not grow deep into the soil. To help support the tree, the roots of several trees grow around each other. When high winds blow, the tangle of roots keeps the redwoods upright.

Redwood trees grow in moist soil. The giant redwoods need plenty of water. Most grow in rainy areas.

FEMALE CONE

scale

SCALE

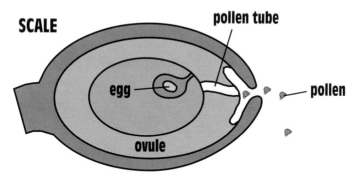

pollen tube

egg

pollen

ovule

Pollen from the male cone floats through the air to a scale of the female cone. Then the pollen enters the ovule through the pollen tube. There, the pollen fertilizes the egg, which grows into a seed.

11

Insects and Other Friends

At least 1,700 different types of animals use the redwood trees for food and shelter. Most are insects, spiders, and **mites**. Many are **pollinators** or **predators** that eat **pests**.

Redwoods also are home for birds and small **mammals.** Many owls, squirrels, and chipmunks nest high within the leaves and branches.

Opposite page: Redwood trees provide homes for many birds and mammals.

Pests and Diseases

Redwood trees do not have a **pest** problem. Their wood is resistant to insects, **disease**—even small fires. This is why some redwoods are over 2,500 years old.

Climate changes, severe forest fires, floods, storms, and people are the biggest problems. The redwoods' shallow roots are easily damaged by road construction. **Logging** once threatened the coast and sequoia redwoods. Laws now protect the redwoods.

Opposite page:
The wood of the redwood tree is resistant to insects and disease.

15

Varieties

Sixty million years ago, over 40 different types of redwoods existed. Today there are only 3 kinds.

The coast redwood grows over 300 feet (91 meters) and is the tallest plant in the world. The sequoia redwood contains the most amount of wood and is the world's largest plant.

The dawn redwood was discovered in China in the 1940s. It is a smaller redwood tree, reaching 70 to 100 feet (21 to 30 meters) tall.

HOUSE
30 ft (9 m)

APPLE TREE
30 ft (9 m)

COTTONWOOD TREE
Over 100 ft (30 m)

REDWOOD TREE
Over 300 ft (91 m)

A dawn redwood tree.

Uses

Redwood trees are cut for lumber used to build homes. The tough, **rot-resistant** wood is used for shingles, siding, fencing, and decking. The **harvested** trees are replaced with **seedlings** for future use.

The older giant trees are rarely cut. Most are protected in state and **federal** parks.

Opposite page:
The older giant redwood trees are
protected in state and federal parks.

Redwood Trees and the Plant Kingdom

The plant kingdom is divided into several groups, including flowering plants, fungi, plants with bare seeds, and ferns.

 Flowering plants grow flowers to make seeds. These seeds often grow inside protective ovaries or fruit.

 Fungi are plants without leaves, flowers, or green coloring, and cannot make their own food. They include mushrooms, molds, and yeast.

 Plants with bare seeds (such as conifers) do not grow flowers. Their seeds grow unprotected, often on the scale of a cone.

 Ferns are plants with roots, stems, and leaves. They do not grow flowers or seeds.

There are two groups of plants with bare seeds: conifers and ginkgos. Conifers grow cones that make seeds. Ginkgos grow fruit that have seeds.

The redwood family is one type of conifer. Coast redwoods, giant sequoias, and dawn redwoods are part of the redwood family.

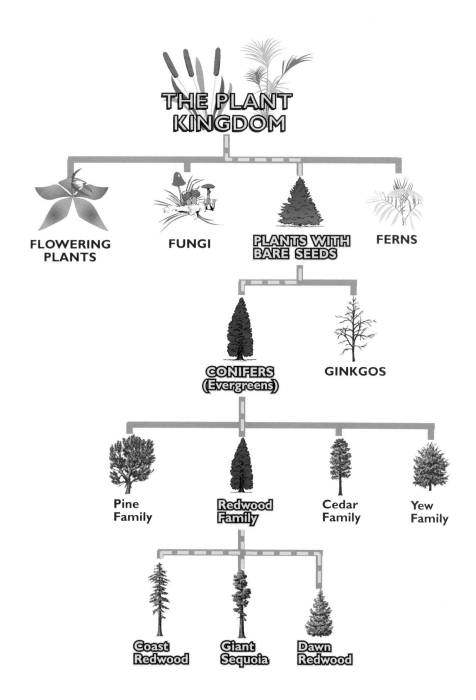

THE PLANT KINGDOM

FLOWERING PLANTS

FUNGI

PLANTS WITH BARE SEEDS

FERNS

CONIFERS (Evergreens)

GINKGOS

Pine Family

Redwood Family

Cedar Family

Yew Family

Coast Redwood

Giant Sequoia

Dawn Redwood

Glossary

bald cypress - A large swamp tree related to the sequoia.

climate (KLIE-mat) - The type of weather a place has.

coniferous (kuh-NIFF-russ) - Referring to cone-bearing plants.

disease (diz-EEZ) - A sickness.

federal (FED-er-ull) - Formed by the central government of the United States; not belonging to any state or city.

fertilize (FUR-tull-eyes) - To make a thing start to grow.

fossil - The hardened remains of something that lived long ago.

harvest - To cut down and gather.

logging - The work of cutting down trees, sawing them into logs, and moving the logs out of the forest.

mammals (MAM-ulz) - A class of animals, including humans, that have hair and feed their young milk.

mineral (MIN-er-ull) - Any substance that is not a plant, animal, or another living thing.

mite - A tiny animal related to the spider and has eight legs.

nutrient (NOO-tree-ent) - Substance that promotes growth or good health.

oxygen (OX-ih-jen) - A gas without color, taste, or odor found in air and water.

pest - A harmful or destructive insect.

photosynthesis (foe-toe-SIN-thuh-sis) - Producing food using sunlight as the source of energy.

pollen (PAH-lin) - A yellow powder that fertilizes flowers.

pollinate (PAH-lin-ate) - To move pollen from flower to flower, allowing them to develop seeds.

pollinator (PAH-lin-ay-tor) - Something that helps pollinate a flower.

predator (PRED-uh-tor) - An animal that eats other animals.

rot-resistant - Withstands diseases or decay.

seedling - A young plant grown from a seed.

Index